HOWARDS END

Notes on English Literature

Chief Adviser: JOHN D. JUMP
*Professor of English Literature in the
University of Manchester*

General Editor: W. H. MASON
Lately Senior English Master, Manchester Grammar School

HOWARDS END

(E. M. FORSTER)

G. P. WAKEFIELD

*Senior English Master, King George V School,
Southport*

BASIL BLACKWELL
OXFORD

0001949 2.

First published in 1968
Reprinted 1970

Printed in Great Britain by Alden & Mowbray Ltd. at
the Alden Press, Oxford, and bound at the Kemp Hall
Bindery, Oxford

CONTENTS

GENERAL NOTE

This series of introductions to the great classics of English literature is designed primarily for the school, college, and university student, although it is hoped that they will be found helpful by a much larger audience. Three aims have been kept in mind:

(A) To give the reader the relevant information necessary for his fuller understanding of the work.

(B) To indicate the main areas of critical interest, to suggest suitable critical approaches, and to point out possible critical difficulties.

(C) To do this in as simple and lucid a manner as possible, avoiding technical jargon and giving a full explanation of any critical terms employed.

Each introduction contains questions on the text and suggestions for further reading. It should be emphasized that in no sense is any introduction to be considered as a substitute for the reader's own study, understanding, and appreciation of the work.

I. PURPOSE

Mention E. M. Forster and most people think immediately of *A Passage to India*, which many would claim to be his masterpiece. The view is certainly arguable, but there are reasons for the outstanding attention that novel has received which have more to do with the circumstances of its publication, in relation both to twentieth-century history and to Forster's own literary career, than with its merit as a work of art. For it was a topical book, a book about race relations—although little penetration is needed to see that it is about a great deal more also—and when it appeared in 1924, the British Raj had still nearly a quarter of a century ahead in India, scarcely changing from the picture Forster had drawn of it. And it was his last novel, separated by fourteen years, and a war that had changed the social even more than the political scene, from the four novels that preceded it. These now seemed dated, and the 'Italian' novels, *Where Angels Fear to Tread* and *A Room with a View* were comparatively slight of stature and appeared too narrowly personal in their attitude, in their themes too limited. The critics had never been at ease with the rather amorphous *The Longest Journey*, and *Howards End* remained in eclipse with the other three. Thus in 1938 Dr. Leavis remarked, somewhat patronizingly, that the pre-war novels are 'the work of a significantly original talent, and they would have deserved to be still read and remembered, even if they had not been the early work of the author of *A Passage to India*'. (*Scrutiny*, VII, reprinted in *The Common Pursuit*, London 1952.) Such a view dies hard, especially when it supports

7

Howards End

opinion based on less critically relevant considerations, of the political topicality and the outwardly more defined issues involved, which directed the general reader's attention to Forster's last novel.

But later years have shown the novels in a different perspective. The situation in India no longer corresponds to that of Forster's Chandrapore and the reader must look a little further below the surface to see the novel's great worth as a study of personal relations, so that now it stands on a more equal footing, certainly in this one respect, with its predecessors; and it is likely to remain there, since human nature does not change in accord with changing manners and the changing political scene. By 1944, Lionel Trilling was able to assert in his influential study of Forster that

> The other literary fact that is likely to influence our feelings about all of Forster's novels is that they are by the author of *Howards End*. This is not to imply a denigration of the other work or to suggest a significant difference in quality. But *Howards End* is undoubtedly Forster's masterpiece.

It is not my purpose, in these introductory comments, to advance a claim that *Howards End*, or indeed any other of the five novels, is Forster's 'best' work. The reader must make his own choice, if he feels the need to do so, and the author himself seems to favour *The Longest Journey*. Rather, I wish to show that all exclusive judgments of this kind have their attendant dangers.

'Only connect . . .', the motto inscribed on the title-page of *Howards End*, might well be applied to all the novels, for it is central to Forster's liberal thinking. In the two 'Italian' novels it is emphasized by the contrast between the repressed, convention-bound life of English society and the natural warmth and uninhibited emotional responsiveness of Italy. *Where Angels Fear to Tread* represents this warmth directly in the person of Gino, and it is Caroline Abbott and Philip Herriton, originally emissaries from Sawston, who are led to understanding through their experience in Italy. In *A Room with a View*, however, there is no major Italian character, but Italy is felt as a mystical influence for good. George Emerson, despite Forster's shadowy portrait of him, embodies this influence in his sincerity and physical attractiveness, so that Lucy Honeychurch finally breaks off her engagement to Cecil Vyse because he is 'the sort that can know no one intimately'. In India, too, Forster saw the need for connection and *A Passage to India* reveals it primarily in the relations between Indians and Anglo-Indians, between Hindus and Moslems and among the English residents of the Chandrapore club. *The Longest Journey*, on the other hand, confines its scene, as *Howards End* does for the most part, to England; the 'only connect' theme, though present, is heard less distinctly, while Forster elaborates others, of the nature of reality, for instance, and the weary tragedy (there is little of Forster's comic spirit here) of those who

The dreariest and the longest journey go

constraining themselves by some narrow alliance when they might reach, through friendship, towards intellectual and imaginative liberation, and the fulfilment of the soul's needs.

But *Howards End* is the only novel of Forster's in which this always present but variously accented theme of the importance of connection, the key to personal relations, is openly dominant, and in Margaret Schlegel, his most fully realized, most convincingly 'round' character, Forster creates the articulate apologist of his own philosophy.

Something should be said about that philosophy, for it is not easy to summarize. In his study of E. M. Forster in the 'Writers and Critics' series, K. W. Gransden has drawn attention to what Forster said about André Gide:

> He has remained an individualist in an age which imposes discipline. . . . He's subtle and elusive.

and again, after Gide's death:

> He had not a great mind. But he had a free mind, and free minds are as rare as great and even more valuable at the present moment.

With justification, Gransden points to some similarity between Gide and Forster himself in this respect, for he too resists the neat label. He is the spokesman for no school and his influence, considerable as it has been during his lifetime, is not that of the militant reformer, the passionate rebel. He is neither a Lawrence nor an Orwell, often though he may be in sympathy with such writers.

The biographical detail relevant to some understanding of Forster's position is generally known and need be only briefly mentioned here. His unhappiness at school and his delight in the intellectual freedom of Cambridge are reflected in *The Longest Journey*. At Cambridge his friends included many of those who were later to become known as the 'Bloomsbury Group'—Leonard and Virginia Woolf, Lytton Strachey, Roger Fry, Bertrand Russell, Maynard Keynes, among others—and though he has disputed the suggestion that he 'belongs' to this group, he was familiar with the work of the philosopher G. E. Moore, the group's acknowledged mentor, whose *Principia Ethica* was published in 1903, soon after Forster had left Cambridge. In the chapter on the 'Ideal', Moore states that 'the pleasures of human intercourse and the enjoyment of beautiful objects' must be considered 'the most valuable things which we can know or imagine'. This is an idea implicit in Forster's writing, but he was not a disciple of Moore's, and in *Howards End* he makes a little gentle fun of his search for what is good 'on the whole' when Margaret is planning to invite Leonard Bast to tea after the Beethoven concert:

> She found him interesting on the whole—everyone interested the Schlegels on the whole at that time. (Chapter V)

The last three words give a hint of Forster's attitude to vogues in philosophy. He came under other influences, too, notably from Goldsworthy Lowes Dickinson, whose biography he was later to write, and from his tutor, the ebullient Nathaniel Wedd. Readers interested in a full account of Forster's Cambridge days will find that Wilfred Stone has provided it in *The Cave and the Mountain*, a critical biography much enhanced by its gleanings from Forster's own reminiscences in conversation with the author.

Forster's sympathies, then, are largely with the liberal tradition, but the idealist in him maintains a dialogue with the realist, even in the last lines of his last novel:

> 'Why can't we be friends now?' said the other, holding him affectionately. 'It's what I want. It's what you want.'

But the horses didn't want it—they swerved apart; the earth didn't want it, sending up rocks through which riders must pass single file; the temples, the tank, the jail, the palace, the birds, the carrion, the Guest House, that came into view as they issued from the gap and saw Mau beneath; they didn't want it, they said in their hundred voices: 'No, not yet,' and the sky said: 'No, not there.'

In *Howards End* Forster applies himself more directly than in any of the other novels to what has come to be known as the class war. Elsewhere, class distinctions of one kind or another had played their part in the action, but rather as an element of the social comedy than as the source of the main conflict; in *A Passage to India*, of course, they appeared in a special context. But an important theme of *Howards End* presents the contrast between the rich and confident world of the Wilcoxes and the near-poverty of Leonard Bast, living 'on the edge of the abyss'. This contrast provides a principal source of action. Early in the novel, however, Forster issues a warning to the reader:

We are not concerned with the very poor. They are unthinkable, and only to be approached by the statistician or the poet. The story deals with gentlefolk, or with those who are obliged to pretend that they are gentlefolk. (Chapter VI)

There is irony here, and failure to detect it has led some critics to indignant comment, but in addition to the irony there is a very helpful signpost. Forster is interested in the welfare of men's minds, which need a more complex ministration than their bodies. He deliberately plays down the dramatic possibilities of the theme of abject poverty. When Helen brings the Basts to Shropshire she tells Margaret that they are starving:

> 'Have you actually brought two starving people from London to Shropshire, Helen?'
> Helen was checked. She had not thought of this, and her hysteria abated. 'There was a restaurant car on the train,' she said.
> 'Don't be absurd. They aren't starving, and you know it. Now, from the beginning. I won't have such theatrical nonsense.' (Chapter XXVI)

Later, Leonard manages to live on the grudging charity of his relatives, after declining Helen's five thousand pounds.

> Unmarried, Leonard would never have begged; he would have flickered out and died. But the whole of life is mixed. He had to provide for Jacky, and went down dirty paths that she might have a few feathers and the dishes of food that suited her. (Chapter XLI)

Therefore, important as the contrast between rich and poor is to the plot, it is the intellectual, emotional and spiritual contrast between people that occupies the centre of the stage, and the leading actors are Schlegels and Wilcoxes.

An illuminating comment on Englishmen of the Wilcox type is to be found in Forster's 'Notes on the English Character' which appear as the first essay in *Abinger Harvest*. Speaking of the effects of a public-school education on Englishmen, he says that they

> go forth into a world that is not entirely composed of public-school men or even of Anglo-Saxons, but of

men who are as various as the sands of the sea; into a world of whose richness and subtlety they have no conception. They go forth into it with well-developed bodies, fairly developed minds, and undeveloped hearts. And it is this undeveloped heart that is largely responsible for the difficulties of Englishmen abroad. An undeveloped heart—not a cold one. The difference is important. . . .

This is what *Howards End* is about. If we are to achieve fulfilment through personal relations, if we are to connect, we must allow our hearts to develop.

The Wilcox world appears to the passionate and sensitive Helen, after her initial encounter with it which is already over when the novel begins, to engender only panic and emptiness. The nightmarish vagueness of this description characterizes her impulsive emotional response; Margaret sees the Wilcoxes in a more rational way:

'To think that because you and a young man meet for a moment, there must be all these telegrams and anger,' supplied Margaret.

Helen nodded.

'I've often thought about it, Helen. It's one of the most interesting things in the world. The truth is that there is a great outer life that you and I have never touched— a life in which telegrams and anger count. Personal relations, that we think supreme, are not supreme there. There love means marriage settlements, death, death duties.' (Chapter IV)

The Wilcoxes belong to what Forster calls 'the civilization of luggage'. They have no roots, they are always on the move. Howards End is merely a property to which they wish to retain their title; Ducie Street and Oniton are convenient halts upon their restless journey, houses occupied and abandoned without emotion. Movables mean more to them, an attitude Forster symbolizes in their worship of the motor-car, the infant pagan deity he had learnt, in 1910, to loathe and fear. He even gives the impassive chauffeur, Crane, the slightly sinister rôle of attendant priest. The day after Mrs. Wilcox's funeral, Charles's heart is heavy as he thinks of his mother, remembering

> How she had disliked improvements, yet how loyally she had accepted them when made! He and his father— what trouble they had had to get this very garage! With what difficulty they had persuaded her to yield them the paddock for it—the paddock that she loved more dearly than the garden itself! (Chapter XI)

Nevertheless, and despite the attempts of his young bride to speak to him, his attention is wholly occupied in cross-questioning Crane about the mud on his new car. Dolly was trying to tell him that his mother had left Howards End to Margaret Schlegel.

The Schlegel world is the antithesis of the Wilcox world. It is the world of music, art, books and a somewhat feverish intellectual activity illustrated by the dinner-party and discussion-group at which a paper was read on 'How ought I to dispose of my money?' The two girls owed much to the example of their father, a German idealist 'the countryman of Hegel and Kant', who naturalized himself in England when he grew weary of his fatherland's expansionism. To a 'haughty nephew' he had said:

'You only care about the things that you can use, and therefore arrange them in the following order: Money, supremely useful; intellect, rather useful; imagination, of no use at all. No'—for the other had protested— 'your Pan-Germanism is no more imaginative than is our imperialism over here.' (Chapter IV)

More important still, the Schlegels are interested in people, and above all they care about them.

These two worlds, then, are presented in contrast with each other, but it is not a simple contrast between obvious right and wrong, between good and evil. Forster will only allow liberal idealism to take him so far. The Wilcoxes are seen to have merit; they are honest and, within their limitations, well intentioned. They are not cruel landlords; there is no grinding of the faces of the poor. They are good administrators: Paul does useful work in Africa, returning there, from a strong sense of duty, even though his health has been threatened. They are, in fact, needed. Their kind provides the money that makes the cultured life of the Schlegels possible, as Margaret points out (to Helen) when she is planning to accept Henry's proposal of marriage:

'If Wilcoxes hadn't worked and died in England for thousands of years, you and I couldn't sit here without having our throats cut. There would be no trains, no ships to carry us literary people about in, no fields even. Just savagery. No—perhaps not even that. Without their spirit life might never have moved out of the protoplasm. More and more do I refuse to draw my income and sneer at those who guarantee it.' (Chapter XIX)

On the other hand, while the Wilcox world has 'grittiness' Margaret feels that her own world has inherent weakness. 'Do personal relations lead to sloppiness in the end?' she asks. It is a dependent world, and at worst its pursuit of culture may become superficial. The sublimity of Beethoven's Fifth Symphony is for Tibby chiefly remarkable for a 'transitional passage on the drum', and Mrs. Wilcox's presence at the luncheon party makes Margaret think of her other guests' brittle conversation as the gibbering of monkeys, though they are her own circle and she has taken part in their talk. The Schlegel sisters themselves, however, are impatient of super-ficiality. That is why they try to check Leonard's out-pourings about books; his walk in the disappointing dawn is what matters to them:

> Within his cramped little mind dwelt something that was greater than Jefferies' books—the spirit that led Jefferies to write them; and his dawn, though revealing nothing but monotones, was part of the eternal sunrise that shows George Borrow Stonehenge. (Chapter XIV)

Furthermore, the mistakes of involvement in personal relations, even more than those of indifference and re-serve, may lead to unhappy consequences, as Helen is to realize, first on Leonard's account and later on her own.

Before we look at some of the ways in which the Wilcoxes fail to 'connect' and the Schlegels attempt to do so, the word should be seen in its context. It is used when Margaret and Henry are preparing for marriage, before the Basts' disastrous arrival at Oniton.

> Margaret greeted her lord with peculiar tenderness on the morrow. Mature as he was, she might yet be able to help him to the building of the rainbow bridge that should connect the prose in us with the passion.

B

> Without it we are meaningless fragments, half monks,
> half beasts, unconnected arches that have never joined
> into a man. With it love is born, and alights on the
> highest curve, glowing against the grey, sober against
> the fire. (Chapter XXII)

There follows a paragraph concerned with Henry's
'incomplete asceticism', with his 'sneaking belief that
bodily passion is bad, a belief that is desirable only
when held passionately'.

> He could not be as the saints and love the Infinite with
> a seraphic ardour, but he could be a little ashamed of
> loving a wife. 'Amabat, amare timebat.' And it was
> here that Margaret hoped to help him. It did not seem
> so difficult. She need trouble him with no gift of her
> own. She would only point out the salvation that was
> latent in his own soul, and in the soul of every man.
> Only connect! That was the whole of her sermon.
> Only connect the prose and the passion, and both will
> be exalted, and human love will be seen at its height.
> Live in fragments no longer. Only connect, and the
> beast and the monk, robbed of the isolation that is
> life to either, will die.

Thus the first and most important connection must be
made within oneself, harmonizing the many chords of
the personality.

The Wilcoxes' failures to connect are all outward
consequences of their failure to achieve the inward
connection. The exclusiveness shown in their attitude to
Paul and Helen; their subterfuge in the matter of Mrs.
Wilcox's bequest of Howards End to Margaret; Henry's
view of Leonard Bast and the Porphyrion affair; his
reaction to Jacky and later to Helen's pregnancy; all these

and others stem from the same root. Of all the Wilcoxes, Charles is the least capable of connection, and it is he who strikes the final blow and who pays the harshest penalty.

Similarly, the Schlegels, who by nature and education have no difficulty in making the inward connection, manifest its influence upon them in their actions— principally Margaret's marriage to Henry and Helen's impetuous sympathy in giving herself to Leonard. They are aware of themselves as part of humanity with responsibilities to others, they recognize the need for affection, they celebrate what Forster, in *Two Cheers for Democracy* has called Love, the Beloved Republic. Therefore Margaret wrote to Helen at an early stage in the novel, soon after Mrs. Wilcox had died:

'Don't brood too much on the superiority of the unseen to the seen. It's true, but to brood on it is medieval. Our business is not to contrast the two, but to reconcile them.' (Chapter XII)

(By 'medieval' Forster does not mean simply 'old-fashioned.' For him it is a special term of disparagement; he saw the spirit of the medieval age as one of narrow restraint, in contrast to classical completeness. In *A Room with a View*, the chapter introducing Cecil Vyse is headed 'Medieval'.)

And so, in concluding this introductory sketch of Forster's purpose in *Howards End*, we see that, following the liberal tradition in general direction, he has also explored by-paths for himself and come to lay the final emphasis on the need for reconciliation, indeed for compromise rather than conquest. A recent essay by H. A. Smith, 'Forster's Humanism and the Nineteenth

Century', published in the Forster volume of 'Twentieth Century Views', has shown that in attacking 'the inner darkness in high places which comes with a commercial age', Forster follows a long succession of writers, some of whom express their humanism in the two voices, romantic and, in a sense, religious, in which he also speaks. Smith draws our attention to Carlyle, Dickens and Arnold; he notes various echoes of Keats's famous statement, 'I am certain of nothing but of the holiness of the heart's affections and the truth of the imagination', that are to be found in Forster's work; he points to Wordsworth's identification in *The Prelude*, of Imagination with 'Intellectual Love'. These writers and others all contributed much to the climate of thought which made Forster's writing possible. But Forster made an original contribution, in that advocacy of reconciliation and compromise which is at once the heart of the matter of *Howards End* and the sinew of his elusive philosophy.

Questions

1. Compare *Howards End* and another novel by Forster as media for expressing his views on life.

2. Discuss and illustrate the relevance of 'Only connect' to *Howards End*.

3. How far are you in sympathy with Forster's particular kind of liberalism? Do the events of the novel provide evidence for challenging it?

4. What allowance do you find you have to make, when reading *Howards End*, for the fact that it was written very early in the twentieth century? If none is necessary, explain why you think so.

II. METHOD

When we consider the methods Forster uses to achieve his purpose we can ask for no better guide than that he provides in *Aspects of the Novel*, for in discussing other people's novels he throws light around the workshop in which his own were fashioned. In this chapter we shall look at the structure and the style of *Howards End*.

Structure

First of all, his well known comment on the importance of the story in a novel:

> Yes—oh dear yes—the novel tells a story. That is the fundamental aspect without which it could not exist. That is the highest factor common to all novels, and I wish that it was not so, that it could be something different—melody, or perception of the truth, not this low atavistic form.

The story, he says, is 'the narrative of events arranged in their time sequence' but

> When we isolate the story . . . from the nobler aspects through which it moves . . . it presents an appearance that is both unlovely and dull.

Daily life, too, relies much on the time sense, but a great deal of its meaning depends rather on value, 'something which is measured not by minutes or hours but by intensity'. The time sequence of a novel may be rearranged (as Conrad so often rearranges it, for example, when he employs what was called his 'indirect method') but it

21

may not be abandoned. Gertrude Stein tried to abandon
it, and Forster says:

> She fails, because as soon as fiction is completely
> delivered from time it cannot express anything at all,
> and in her later writing we can see the slope down
> which she is slipping.

Turning from story to plot, Forster challenges Aristotle's view that all human happiness and misery take the
form of action:

> We know better. We believe that happiness and misery
> exist in the secret life, which each of us leads privately
> and to which (in his characters) the novelist has access.

Thus he observes that the plot,

> instead of finding human beings more or less cut to
> its requirements, as they are in the drama, finds them
> enormous, shadowy, and intractable, and three-
> quarters hidden like an iceberg.

He continues:

> A plot is also a narrative of events, the emphasis falling
> on causality.

To understand the plot, then, we must use intelligence
and memory, intelligence to grasp the novelist's purpose,
for instance in his use of mystery and surprise, and
memory to store up all the novelist provides for our
intelligence to assess.

> Every action or word in a plot ought to count; it ought
> to be economical and spare; even when complicated it
> should be organic and free from dead matter. It may be
> difficult or easy, it may and should contain mysteries, but

it ought not to mislead. And over it, as it unfolds, will hover the memory of the reader (that dull glow of the mind of which intelligence is the bright advancing edge) and will constantly rearrange and reconsider, seeing new clues, new chains of cause and effect, and the final sense (if the plot has been a fine one) will not be of clues or chains, but of something aesthetically compact, something which might have been shown by the novelist straight away, only if he had shown it straight away it would never have become beautiful.

He draws attention to the novelist's use of shock, to the conflict which arises between character and plot and to the difficulties so often encountered in the conclusion:

If it was not for death and marriage I do not know how the average novelist would conclude.

In applying these ideas to *Howards End* we can see at once a striking contrast between its story and its plot. The story (there is no need to weary the reader with a summary) is a straightforward account of what happens to the Schlegel sisters as a result of their meeting the Wilcoxes and Leonard Bast. It includes unexpected death, marriage, passing sexual encounter and violence; coincidences occur and once or twice the events are melodramatic. Situation follows situation, as in real life, in the inevitable unrolling of the scroll of time. We are introduced to these people at one point on the scroll, we follow their fortunes for a while, and we leave them at a later point. Stories have no meaning; they merely show what happens next and their power to hold our interest depends to a great extent on surprise, coincidence and improbability. Once we cease to wonder we become bored. So Forster surprises us: when Helen breaks off her engagement to Paul, for instance, when Mrs. Wilcox dies, when Helen becomes pregnant, when Charles strikes Leonard with the sword. He includes coincidence: it is a coincidence that the Wilcoxes should take a flat opposite the Schlegels' house in Wickham Place, that Jacky should have been Mr. Wilcox's mistress, that Leonard should arrive at Howards End just when everyone's emotions have been strained by Helen's return in distressing circumstances. And he does not shrink from including improbability: is it probable, we ask, that Helen should give herself sexually to Leonard, or that Margaret should marry Mr. Wilcox? When we try to answer questions such as this, or to see what has been surprising or coincidental in due perspective, the story is of no help to us. We must think about the plot. What we have described as Forster's purpose in *Howards End* must appear through the plot, for the plot is concerned with happiness and misery, with the shadowy nature of people, the part of the iceberg that is not visible. It therefore directs the course and shape of the story, so as to make clear the author's themes and his judgment of values.

The plot of *Howards End* is more difficult to summarize than the story, but some attempt must be made. Two young women of liberal education and developed sensibilities try to come to terms with society. Their consciences are active about their place in society, about their relations with people who have enjoyed fewer advantages than they themselves have, such as Leonard Bast, or who have less sensibility but more money and power, such as the Wilcoxes. They are much concerned with the question of money—of its use and abuse—and with the part played in life by love, sex, prejudice, enthusiasm, indifference. It is in such terms as these that the plot must be considered.

The most obvious feature of the plot is its structural dependence on the Schlegel sisters, and particularly on Margaret, just as that of *Pride and Prejudice* depends on Elizabeth Bennet, that of *Great Expectations* depends on Pip, and that of *Tess of the d'Urbervilles* on Tess. Compare these novels in this respect with, say, *Middlemarch*, in which the plot is unfolded not only from Dorothea Brooke's viewpoint, but from Lydgate's, Ladislaw's, Fred Vincy's, even Bulstrode's; or *A Tale of Two Cities* (Darnay, Carton, Manet and others); or *The Return of the Native* (Eustacia, Clym, Thomasin). We may also notice that in the two novels by Dickens the story is more important than the plot, whereas in the other examples it is not so. Forster's *A Passage to India* is not constructed around one central character, for our attention is focused sometimes on Aziz, sometimes on Adela, Fielding or even on less important characters. There are scenes in *Howards End* when neither Schlegel girl is present—at the Basts', or quite often within the Wilcox family—but their influence is always important to these scenes. There is only one fleeting moment when Mrs. Wilcox is seen with her family in a purely Wilcox setting, at King's Cross, and even then Margaret is there as a bystander. This little incident is highly charged with irony and meaning.

The structure of *Howards End*, then, must be examined in relation to both the story and the plot and it will be seen that each proceeds through a series of climaxes, some of them crises, each climax having its special significance in the exposition of Forster's purpose.

(1) The affair of Helen and Paul (Chapters I–IV). Forster begins with a crisis, arresting our attention at once, and changing its nature dramatically with the arrival of Helen's telegram at the end of Chapter II. But this novel is not to be about Helen and Paul, and the crisis is important to the establishment of our first ideas about the Schlegels and the Wilcoxes, not to the subsequent course of events, though its consequences are felt from time to time. The Schlegels and the Wilcoxes are linked, even though in hostility. We are shown Helen's impetuousness, Margaret's greater maturity and sense of the proportions of things, and (subtly, through the letters) something of their relationship with each other. We are shown the Wilcox world, again through the letters, and the Wilcox behaviour at its worst when Charles meets Mrs. Munt at the station. And so we move on, to the idea of panic and emptiness, of telegrams and anger, one aspect of the world around them with which the liberal, 'intellectual' Schlegels have come to terms. Not least, it scarcely need be said, the episode introduces us to Howards End and to its *genius loci*, Ruth Wilcox.

(2) The umbrella episode (Chapters V and VI). This, of course, introduces the second main aspect of society with which the Schlegels are to have dealings, the world of those who, like Leonard Bast, 'stood at the extreme verge of gentility'.

> He was not in the abyss, but he could see it, and at times people whom he knew had dropped in, and counted no more.

In the preceding four chapters the tone of social comedy has already been heard, but now it is modulated, first at the concert and again in Leonard's flat. (The ironic whimsicality of the Beethoven references will be discussed later, when Forster's style is considered.)

(3) The death of Ruth Wilcox (Chapters VII–XII). Here Forster uses the 'shock' device that he is to use several times again in this novel and that he frequently uses elsewhere. Notable examples are the death of Gino's child in *Where Angels Fear to Tread*; 'Gerald died that afternoon' in *The Longest Journey;* and the arrest of Aziz in *A Passage to India*. Careful reading, however, shows that these shocks are often prepared for. Early in Chapter VIII there is a hint: 'Mrs. Wilcox has left few clear indications behind her', and when Margaret called she found her taking a day in bed. 'Now and then I do', she said, and later, 'The truth is I am a little tired.' At King's Cross, a few lines from the end of Chapter X, Henry asked 'How's yourself, Ruth?' The irony of her reply,

'Fit as a fiddle,' she answered gaily,

is immediately apparent when Chapter XI opens with the words: 'The funeral was over.' (Forster frequently drops hints, unnoticed on a first reading, about events to come, whether or not they are to come as shocks. Here, in Chapter VII, is Mrs. Munt commenting on what she has seen of the Wilcoxes in the flat opposite to Wickham Place:

'And who would an elderly man with a moustache and a copper-coloured face be?'
'Mr. Wilcox, possibly.'
'I knew it. And there's Mr. Wilcox.'
'It's a shame to call his face copper colour,' complained Margaret. 'He has a remarkably good complexion for a man of his age.')

Mrs. Wilcox's death leads directly to another crisis in the Wilcox household, that occasioned by the discovery of her letter bequeathing Howards End to Margaret. During these chapters one or two subsidiary themes have been introduced: the relentless flux of London in which houses are destroyed to make way for blocks of flats, and the idea that a house has a life, a spirit of its own.

In the next chapters (XIII–XVI) the movement slows down, and although there is the scene of Leonard's violent reaction to the Schlegels' attempt to advise him about the Porphyrion Fire Insurance Company, no crisis or climax advances the story. Events are taken up after an interval of two years and this part of the novel is used to expand various themes: London, the loss of a home, Tibby; the use and misuse of literary culture is discussed in relation to Leonard's talk about books, and the women's discussion group furthers the subject of the responsibility of possessing money. Movement begins again when, after the discussion, the Schlegels meet Mr. Wilcox on Chelsea embankment, for this prepares the way for Leonard's disintegration and Margaret's marriage. Helen's attitude towards both Leonard and Henry develops a stage further.

(4) The fourth important climax is Henry's proposal of marriage to Margaret (Chapters XVII–XXIV). Now a conflict of feeling, rather than of will, grows between Margaret and Helen, aggravated still more by Henry's change of attitude over the Porphyrion affair. Finally, this movement brings Margaret to Howards End for the first time, an incident notable principally for Miss Avery's mistaking her for Ruth Wilcox, a suggestion of the spiritual rôle Forster ascribes to the house.

In the remainder of the novel, a little over a third of

the whole, the climaxes follow one another more rapidly, and all are crises. They need be only briefly indicated.

(5) The arrival of the Basts at Oniton (Chapters XXV–XXIX). In this crisis Margaret is called upon to practise, in the most exacting circumstances, what she has preached in her 'sermon'. 'Would she really have married Henry Wilcox?' people ask, seeking to find Forster in error. But he had spoken, in *Aspects of the Novel*, of 'the countless examples in which either plot or character has to suffer', and of the example he cited from Meredith he said 'Meredith with his unerring good sense here lets the plot triumph.' So does Forster. After the discovery that Jacky has been Henry's mistress, Margaret's marriage is not a question of probability, but of necessity.

(6) Helen's return (Chapters XXX–XXXVIII). The sisters' idyll and the scene of Margaret's great confrontation of Henry.

(7) Leonard's death (Chapters XXXIX–XLIII). Events lead inevitably, through Margaret's decision to leave Henry and his spiritual collapse when Charles is imprisoned, to Howards End, which thus ultimately fulfils its purpose in Forster's philosophical scheme and justifies the novel's title.

The last chapter (XLIV) has been criticized on the grounds that its symbolism is a little too facile. Forster has warned us that conclusions are always difficult and often disappointing. Whatever we may think of this conclusion, its function is to reconcile, to reach a compromise, and it is faithfully performed. Everything else is irrelevant.

It has been possible to show here only the general lines of the structure of *Howards End*. These lines are clearly drawn and serve to express Forster's themes directly, but they are the framework for a finely organized whole, in which every detail has a necessary function. The reader will be rewarded again and again by considering such passages as the conclusion to Chapter XXV, when Charles has observed Margaret alone in the dark meadow at Oniton:

'That woman means mischief', thought Charles, and compressed his lips. In a few minutes he followed her indoors, as the ground was getting damp. Mists were rising from the river, and presently it became invisible, though it whispered more loudly. There had been a heavy downpour in the Welsh hills.

Style

Forster's style, like any other writer's, is not just a matter of the shape and texture of his prose, but before considering the style of *Howards End* in the wider sense, we should look at it for a moment in the narrower.

Forster has sometimes been criticized for employing too much easy colloquialism, especially in the later essays, though many will find there a pleasing informality, unpretentious and direct, reflecting the man himself. In *Howards End*, however, he uses a true familiar style, flexible to his purpose. The conversational tone is heard at once—

'One may as well begin with Helen's letters to her sister'—and it recurs from time to time in the verbless sentence—'Only disobeying them in the letter, surely', 'Also the rent', 'Thus much from his card'—or in the idiomatic phrase: 'But here was Dolly, dressed up to the nines.' Nevertheless, though the style is never stiff and formal, Forster relaxes to this extent only on occasions when his theme suggests that it is appropriate for him to do so.

Of his imagery, which is often striking, and at its best when slightly pejorative, it will suffice to quote a few examples:

> The air was white, and when they alighted it tasted like cold pennies.
>
> A woman of undefinable rarity was going up heavenward, like a specimen in a bottle.
>
> We fellows smoked in chairs of maroon leather. It was as if a motor-car had spawned.
>
> She looked at the scenery. It heaved and merged like porridge. Presently it congealed. They had arrived.
>
> The shadow of the house gathered itself together, and fell over the garden.

The last quotation exemplifies the way in which Forster seeks the life behind inanimate objects, especially in passages of sustained description. Of London he says:

> One visualizes it as a tract of quivering grey, intelligent without purpose, and excitable without love: as a spirit that has altered before it can be chronicled; as a heart that certainly beats, but with no pulsation of humanity. (Chapter XIII)

Or again, as Margaret is driven towards Oniton:

> Shropshire had not the reticence of Hertfordshire. Though robbed of half its magic by swift movement, it still conveyed the sense of hills. They were nearing the buttresses that force the Severn eastward and make

it an English stream, and the sun, sinking over the Sentinels of Wales, was straight in their eyes. . . . Quiet mysteries were in progress behind those tossing horizons: the West, as ever, was retreating with some secret which may not be worth the discovery, but which no practical man will ever discover. (Chapter XXV)

And describing Oniton:

Close to the castle was a grey mansion, unintellectual but kindly, stretching with its grounds across the peninsula's neck—the sort of mansion that was built all over England in the beginning of the last century, while architecture was still an expression of the national character. (Chapter XXV)

Of Oxford:

Perhaps it wants its inmates to love it rather than to love one another. (Chapter XII)

And here is Margaret's arrival at Howards End:

Then the car turned away, and it was as if a curtain had risen. For the second time that day she saw the appearance of the earth.
. . . She must have interviewed Charles in another world, where one did have interviews. How Helen would revel in such a notion! Charles dead, all people dead, nothing alive but houses and gardens. The obvious dead, the intangible alive, and—no connection at all between them! (Chapter XXIII)

In pursuing Forster's imagery we have encroached some-what on the second, wider aspect of style, for this feeling for the intangible quality of countryside, of towns and of houses is more than the evocative use of word and phrase, but before we pass on to this second aspect let us look at Forster's style in dialogue.

Here the flexibility is seen most clearly, for he adapts his style to suit the character of the speaker so that there is no difficulty, as sometimes there is in other novelists' work—Ivy Compton-Burnett's, for example—in distinguishing one speaker from another. Helen is always recognizable: 'One must learn to distinguish tother from which'; 'the wiggly hotel'; 'Bags I writing to Aunt Juley about this. Now, Meg, remember—bags I.' She strikes the same note again even in the later scenes, when her experience has sobered much of her speech to unaccustomed gravity: 'Oh, Meg lovely, do let's.' It is interesting to compare Margaret's manner when, more rarely than Helen, she adopts a light tone. Here she is at Simpson's, talking to Henry about Mr. Eustace Miles's restaurant:

> 'It's all proteids and body buildings, and people come up to you and beg your pardon, but you have such a beautiful aura.'
> 'A what?'
> 'Never heard of an aura? Oh, happy, happy man! I scrub at mine for hours. Nor of an astral plane?' (Chapter XVII)

Evie normally speaks in a somewhat boisterous style, like a forthright schoolgirl: 'Dolly is a rotter not to be here.' Henry's formal, businesslike speech is given overtones of bluff good-humour:

> 'I used to go out for sport and business to Cyprus; some military society of a sort there. A few piastres,

C

properly distributed, help to keep one's memory green.
But you, of course, think this shockingly cynical.
How's your discussion society getting on? Any new
Utopias lately? (Chapter XVII)

Charles, too, is usually rather stiff, and more often tetchy
than good-humoured:

'I hope that my wife—how do you do?—will give
you a decent lunch. I left instructions but we live in a
rough-and-ready way. She expects you back to tea, too,
after you have had a look at Howards End. I wonder
what you'll think of the place. I wouldn't touch it with
tongs myself. Do sit down! It's a measly little place.'
(Chapter XXIII)

The afterthought greeting to his future stepmother is a
revealing touch of characterization. Forster is less successful with Leonard, especially in the scenes with Jacky,
where the flatness is a little overstressed:

'I met Mr. Cunningham outside, and we passed a
few remarks.'
'What, not Mr. Cunningham?'
'Yes.'
'Oh, you mean Mr. Cunningham.'
'Yes. Mr. Cunningham.'

And again:

'My word's my word. I've promised to marry you
as soon as ever I'm twenty-one, and I can't keep on
being worried. I've worries enough. It isn't likely I'd
throw you over, let alone my word, when I've spent
all this money. Besides, I'm an Englishman, and I
never go back on my word.' (Chapter VI)

An important comment of Forster's on the wider aspects of style is given in the passage already quoted from *Aspects of the Novel* referring to clues and chains of cause and effect. He uses frequent repetition of words and phrases which serves both to help the reader in following the clues and chains and to attune him to the novel's underlying rhythms. Some of these repetitions, central to the theme, are obvious at first reading: 'telegrams and anger', 'panic and emptiness' and those sinister goblins, suggested by Beethoven's Fifth Symphony, 'walking quietly over the universe'.

> They were not aggressive creatures; it was that that made them so terrible to Helen. They merely observed in passing that there was no such thing as splendour or heroism in the world.

They appear again, after Jacky's visit to Wickham Place:

> Mrs. Lanoline had risen out of the abyss, like a faint smell, a goblin football, telling of a life where love and hatred had both decayed.

And just before Leonard's death their quiet walk has assumed more malevolence, subtly suggested by a change of verb:

> Again and again must the drums tap, and the goblins stalk over the universe before joy can be purged of the superficial.

The goblins have strayed from the world of fantasy, where Forster enjoys an occasional excursion, and they provide a convenient symbol for militant apathy towards the human situation, if the paradox may be allowed. But Forster takes his symbols from everyday things, too.

Notable among these is the motor-car, and although at
first we may be inclined to dismiss the many references
to it as no more than a sensitive man's distaste, in 1910,
for noise and smell and the relentless pressures of material
progress against man's natural inheritance, we gradually
realize that Forster wishes us to see it as much more.
It is the talisman of Wilcoxism. Ford and Morris had not
yet set up their mass-production lines, and only rich
people had cars. Today even Leonard Bast has a car.
Some references have been noted already and they are
nearly always hostile:

such life as is conferred by the stench of motor-cars;
Mrs. Wilcox

turned to her elder son, who stood still in the throb-
bing, stinking car, and smiled at him with tenderness,
and without saying a word, turned away from him
towards her flowers.

London suffers, as

month by month the roads smelt more strongly of
petrol, and were more difficult to cross, and human
beings heard each other with great difficulty. (Chapter
XIII)

A motor-drive, a form of felicity detested by Margaret,
awaited her. (Chapter XXIII)

And one of Margaret's memories of Evie's wedding was
of 'motor-cars oozing grease on the gravel'. As she arrives
at Waterloo, approaching the moment of Henry's marriage
proposal, there is a note of forbearance, in harmony with
the theme of connection and compromise:

She lingered to admire the motor, which was new,

and a fairer creature than the vermilion giant that had borne Aunt Juley to her doom three years before.

But the price of compromise has soon to be paid. On the journey to Oniton a cat is run over, Charles refuses to stop and Margaret jumps straight out of the car.

Another image contributing to the novel's rhythmic pattern involves the idea of flux and tide, the movement of rivers and sea. Sometimes the references are literal, to the Thames at Chelsea, the sea in Poole harbour and the falling rain. Sometimes one senses a deeper meaning. At the end of Helen's long conversation with Leonard in the empty coffee-room of the Shropshire hotel, Chapter XXVII concludes:

> Presently the waitress entered and gave her a letter from Margaret. Another note, addressed to Leonard, was inside. They read them, listening to the murmurings of the river.

Yet again, some allusions are openly metaphorical, as when he speaks of 'the grey tides of London', or of its demolition and rebuilding:

> bricks and mortar rising and falling with the restlessness of the water in a fountain, as the city receives more and more men upon her soil (Chapter VI);

or when Margaret talks of Helen and herself standing upon money as upon islands, whereas most of the others are down below the surface of the sea. The idea of the rainbow bridge itself, 'connecting the prose in us with the passion', is surely of a span across the separating flood. Much of this echoes a familiar theme of Matthew Arnold's to whom Forster is also indebted for the concept of seeing life steadily and seeing it whole, a theme on which there are recurrent variations.

There are many other examples of clues and chains— 'hands on the ropes', 'inherit the earth', 'hay fever' and words such as love, reality, immortality, light, darkness, grey, the unseen—but the reader must not be denied the satisfaction of discovering them. He may never discover them all, but he will find that Forster has not failed his own artistic criteria, for the final sense is not of clues or chains but 'of something aesthetically compact.' Style and structure are fused together.

They also appear as two aspects of the same thing when we examine Forster's dramatic method. In recent years several of his novels, including *Howards End*, have been adapted for the stage with some success, despite thematic loss due to compression. After the opening letters, the whole episode of Mrs. Munt's visit to Howards End is developed with a strong dramatic sense, and her encounter with Charles builds up through politeness and misunderstanding to a first-class row. To this, on their arrival at the house, the appearance of Mrs. Wilcox 'trailing noiselessly over the lawn' provides a striking contrast and a moving diminuendo:

> 'Mother', he called, 'are you aware that Paul has been playing the fool again?'
> 'It is all right, dear. They have broken off the engagement.'
> 'Engagement—!'
> 'They do not love any longer, if you prefer it put that way', said Mrs. Wilcox, stooping down to smell a rose.

Scene after scene in the novel is conceived in comparably dramatic terms and to what has been said of the flexibility of Forster's dialogue a note must be added on its dramatic effectiveness. Here is Helen, anxious not to embarrass Leonard, whose umbrella she has accidentally taken:

> 'No, I can't remember what I was going to say. That wasn't it, but do tell the maids to hurry tea up. What about this umbrella?' She opened it. 'No, it's all gone along the seams. It's an appalling umbrella. It must be mine.'
>
> But it was not.
>
> He took it from her, murmured a few words of thanks, and then fled, with the lilting step of the clerk. (Chapter V)

Beneath the triviality we sense the tension and the pathos. On their shopping expedition Margaret has helped Mrs. Wilcox to choose a Christmas card and submitted one for her inspection:

> Mrs. Wilcox was delighted—so original, words so sweet; she would order a hundred like that, and could never be sufficiently grateful. Then, just as the assistant was booking the order, she said: 'Do you know, I'll wait. On second thoughts, I'll wait. There's plenty of time still, isn't there, and I shall be able to get Evie's opinion.'
>
> They returned to the carriage by devious paths; when they were in, she said: 'But couldn't you get it renewed?'
>
> 'I beg your pardon?' asked Margaret.
>
> 'The lease, I mean.'
>
> 'Oh, the lease! Have you been thinking of that all the time? How very kind of you!' (Chapter X)

Or at Simpson's with Henry:

> 'Tell me, though, Miss Schegel, do you really believe
> in the supernatural and all that?'
> 'Too difficult a question.'
> 'Why's that? Gruyère or Stilton?'
> 'Gruyère, please.'
> 'Better have Stilton.'
> 'Stilton. Because, though I don't believe in auras. . . .'
> (Chapter XVII)

Forster does not hesitate to suggest mystery, even an
almost supernatural touch, to heighten the drama.
Margaret, alone in the empty Howards End, while the
rain falls heavily, hears a noise within and, thinking it is
Henry, she calls out to him.

> There was no answer, but the house reverberated
> again.
> 'Henry, have you got in?'
> But it was the heart of the house beating, faintly at
> first, then loudly, martially. It dominated the rain.
> It is the starved imagination, not the well-nourished,
> that is afraid. Margaret flung open the door to the
> stairs. A noise as of drums seemed to deafen her. A
> woman, an old woman, was descending, with figure
> erect, with face impassive, with lips that parted and
> said dryly:
> 'Oh! Well, I took you for Ruth Wilcox.'
> Margaret stammered: 'I—Mrs. Wilcox—I?'
> 'In fancy, of course—in fancy. You had her way
> of walking. Good day.' And the old woman passed out
> into the rain. (Chapter XXIII)

The outward mystery is easily dispelled by Henry:

'silly old Miss Avery—she frightened you, didn't she, Margaret?'

But the inner mystery, Forster's deeper concern, is heightened as Henry continues, unwittingly:

'There you stood clutching a bunch of weeds.' (Chapter XXIV)

Two quite different qualities of Forster's style need to be mentioned only briefly, not because they are unimportant, but because they are self-evident. They are his fondness for long descriptive passages and his didacticism. The first, especially notable in his pictures of London and the countryside around Howards End, Swanage and Oniton, provides opportunity for the exercise of poetic imagination; the second is used to extend points of view relevant to the novel's themes. It never degenerates into sermonizing and is often expressed in memorable phrase:

We are evolving, in ways that Science cannot measure, to ends that Theology dares not contemplate.

or

Death destroys a man, but the idea of death saves him.

It is easy to find fifty or sixty examples. Both these qualities are a little out of fashion today and some readers find them obtrusive. My own view is that the book is richer for their inclusion.

Finally, a word on Forster's humour. It is a critical commonplace to speak of his novels as social comedies, and while this description is less appropriate to *Howards End* than to *Where Angels Fear to Tread* and *A Room with a*

View, many of the passages quoted as illustration in other contexts have also revealed the true comic spirit. It is always difficult, and for a critic often unwise, to point specifically to humorous passages, for most humour, like a butterfly's wing, is easily damaged if it is handled, and Forster's humour is of a particularly delicate kind. Nevertheless, the reader will find profit in considering the variety of humorous techniques in the novel. Many of the portraits, especially of minor characters, provide examples. Sometimes the effect is gained by Forster's objective comments, as when we are told that Mrs. Munt 'rehearsed her mission' to Howards End 'most complacently', or that she deplored investment in 'Foreign Things'. Helen, on the other hand, illustrates Forster's skill in creating a character who has a spontaneous sense of fun, and in Leonard's portrait humour and pathos are often yoked together. Even the darkest moments of the novel have their touches of comedy:

> Mr. Wilcox reappeared at eleven, looking very tired. There was to be an inquest on Leonard's body to-morrow, and the police required his son to attend.
>
> 'I expected that,' said Charles. 'I shall naturally be the most important witness there.' (Chapter XLII)

Comic scenes are never introduced merely for their own sake; there is always an underlying relevance to the main theme. Forster sustains the spirit of comedy throughout a number of important episodes, however, such as the luncheon-party for Mrs. Wilcox, Helen's account of 'Mrs. Lanoline's' call, the visit to Simpson's restaurant and the events attendant on Evie's wedding, enlivened by glimpses of the Warringtons, the Fussells and the Italian chauffeur. Yet it is not principally through such scenes that Forster's sense of humour is apparent. Rather, it is a presence pervading all the writing. Sometimes it is half-concealed in understatement:

> Here Beethoven, after humming and hawing with great sweetness, said 'Heigho', and the Andante came to an end. (Chapter V)

or, of Charles reporting Leonard's death to Mr. Wilcox:

> It was no fun doing errands for his father, who was never quite satisfied. (Chapter XIII)

Sometimes it lurks in innuendo:

> Even the Bible—the Dutch Bible that Charles had brought back from the Boer War—fell into position. Such a room admitted loot. (Chapter XVIII)

And sometimes it laughs aloud:

> Evie heard of her father's engagement when she was in for a tennis tournament, and her play went simply to pot. (Chapter XXV)

Wherever it occurs, it is inseparable from Forster's attitude to the human condition. He, too, strives to see life steadily, and see it whole. Comedy and tragedy are kindred spirits.

Questions

1. Choose one or two short passages from the text (about half a page in length) and examine their importance to the novel.

2. Under what circumstances, if any, do you consider

Forster's view, 'that either plot or character sometimes has to suffer', to be justified?

3. Consider the weakness and strength of *Howards End* as a vehicle for expressing Forster's ideas.

4. Write an essay on the variety of Forster's style in *Howards End*.

5. 'I think *Howards End* is all right. But I sometimes get a little bored with it. There seems too much, too many social nuances there.' (E. M. Forster, on his eightieth birthday.) Discuss.

III. CHARACTERS

Once again, let us start with *Aspects of the Novel*:

> There are in the novel two forces: human beings and a bundle of various things not human beings . . . it is the novelist's business to adjust these two forces and conciliate their claims.

For if characters

> are given complete freedom they kick the book to pieces, and if they are kept too sternly in check, they revenge themselves by dying, and destroy it by intestinal decay.

When we think about the characters in *Howards End* we must bear in mind this declaration of rights, theirs and their author's.

Some attempt has been made so far to show what the 'bundle of things' in this novel consists of. It is a typical Forster phrase, unpretentious and disarming, and it suggests with calculated imprecision what he would have us look for, in his own novels at least. It is not a philosophy; philosophy, yes, but not a philosophy. The novel is not the place to develop a system of thought and to make the attempt would lead inevitably to 'intestinal decay'. Rather, we should look for what Arnold called 'a criticism of life', necessary to the novel as it is to poetry, or what Forster himself has described as the song of the prophet.

Forster's famous distinction between 'flat' and 'round' characters—he was not the first to notice this distinction, but he expresses it with great clarity—serves as another useful guide:

> The really flat character can be expressed in one sentence such as 'I will never desert Mr. Micawber.' There is Mrs. Micawber—she says she won't desert Mr. Micawber; she doesn't, and there she is.

The round character, on the other hand, is always capable of surprising us in a convincing way. The novelist cannot make all his characters seem round—if he attempted to do so he would never finish his novel—and so there are plenty of flat characters to be found in Forster's work. There are the Miss Alans in *A Room with a View*, Mrs. Herriton in *Where Angels Fear to Tread*, Mr. Pembroke in *The Longest Journey* and the Turtons and Burtons and their friends in the Chandrapore club in *A Passage to India*, to name a few. And in *Howards End* Jacky is flat, so flat that one critic (C. B. Cox: *The Free Spirit*, Oxford University Press, 1963) maintains that she is hardly a character at all, since she never emerges from the world of melodrama. Evie and Charles and Dolly are other examples. Among the advantages Forster recognizes in flat characters, the most important is that the author has not to watch them for development. But the principal characters are all round; here and in *A Passage to India* Forster gathers together his most convincing portraits.

His method of introducing his characters owes little to nineteenth-century models, a point easily overlooked today since the majority of modern novelists adopt a similar method. He does not begin with a description or an account of their situation at the novel's outset. They are obliged to work their way in through the action as it develops. In the last paragraphs of Chapter IV he gives quite a long account of the origin of the Schlegel girls, but it is a glimpse of their father and of their childhood, a 'flashback' to the past, not a snapshot of the present. Nor does he say much about physical appearance; the occasional hint suffices. Aunt Juley, we have seen, notices Mr. Wilcox's moustache and his 'copper-coloured' face. We are told that Helen is pretty, but we never see her face or her figure, though we are permitted to look at the unimportant Evie for a moment:

> Dark-eyed, with a glow of youth under sunburn, built firmly and firm-lipped, she was the best the Wilcoxes could do in the way of feminine beauty. (Chapter XVI)

This descriptive detail, fuller than that allowed to most of the characters, appears to have been included not so much for its own sake, as to make an ironic comment upon what Evie has just replied to her father's hopeful enquiry ('You like them, don't you, Evie?'):

> 'Helen's right enough, but I can't stand the toothy one.'

That malicious but doubtless factual assessment of Margaret's appearance (Forster had said 'her figure was meagre, her face seemed all teeth and eyes') is about all we have, except that she takes to wearing pince-nez.

Margaret is the most important character in the novel and the chief exponent of Forster's main theme. In this, she is unique in his work. Lucy Honeychurch and Rickie Elliot hold central positions around which the novels they appear in are constructed, but they do not express Forster in the way Margaret does. At first, however, she plays a subsidiary role, as observer and commentator, a mentor to Helen who promises to be the character on whom our interest is to be focused. Nevertheless, we are shown her spiritual maturity and fine sensibility in a series of little touches. At the concert, while Mrs. Munt taps surreptitiously, while Tibby follows the score, Fraulein Mosebach remembers that Beethoven is German and Helen 'sees heroes and shipwrecks in the music's flood', Margaret 'can only see the music'. She is more restrained than Helen. When Leonard remarks that it is a fine programme, she refuses to enthuse, though mere politeness would have allowed her to agree with him; and when, during the walk back to Wickham place, he speaks of attending the gallery for the Royal Opera, she is compared directly with her sister:

> Helen would have exclaimed, 'So do I. I love the gallery', and thus have endeared herself to the young man. Helen could do these things. But Margaret had an almost morbid horror of 'drawing people out', of 'making things go'. She had been to the gallery at Covent Garden, but she did not 'attend' it, preferring the more expensive seats; still less did she love it. So she made no reply. (Chapter V)

Yet she is always considerate; she cannot bear her brother to be scolded.

She distrusts excessive caution and refuses to panic with Aunt Juley when the Wilcoxes arrive at Wickham Mansions. 'She felt that those who prepare for all the emergencies of life beforehand may equip themselves at the expense of joy.' She tells her aunt that she hopes to risk things all her life. She is not as impulsive as Helen, but she is seized by impulses over which she deliberates, and when she does act she hits out 'as lustily as if she had not considered the matter at all'. So it is that she writes

to Mrs. Wilcox to say that it would be better if they did
not meet.

At this point Margaret moves to stage centre, and the
mysterious fusion of her spirit with Mrs. Wilcox's begins.
Earlier, at Speyer, Mrs. Wilcox 'may have detected in
the other and less charming of the sisters a deeper
sympathy, a sounder judgment', and in the few oppor-
tunities that remain before Mrs. Wilcox dies—the bedside
conversation, the luncheon party and the shopping
expedition—a fragile intimacy develops. Afterwards she
feels that Mrs. Wilcox's death has helped her in her work
of trying 'to pierce the accretions in which body and
soul are enwrapped'. She realizes the force that exists in
the Wilcox life:

> She could not despise it, as Helen and Tibby affected
> to do. It fostered such virtues as neatness, decision
> and obedience, virtues of the second rank, no doubt,
> but they have formed our civilization. They form
> character, too; Margaret could not doubt it: they keep
> the soul from becoming sloppy. (Chapter XII)

The final comment before the two years interval between
Chapters XII and XIII is that Margaret hoped she would
be less cautious, not more cautious, than she had been in
the past.

We now approach the central problem of Margaret's
character; her marriage to Henry Wilcox, which has
caused some critics so much misgiving, and of which
F. R. Leavis declares outright: 'Nothing in the exhibition
of Margaret's or Henry Wilcox's character makes the
marriage credible or acceptable.' (*The Common Pursuit*.)
It is the central point at which the claims of character and
plot have to be reconciled. We have already seen that once

D

Jacky has revealed her former liaison with Henry, Forster must proceed with the marriage; but has he up to this crisis made us feel that the mutual attraction, of two people so opposed to each other in situation and purpose, was probable, if not inevitable? The reader must decide for himself, but two considerations are important in reaching the decision. First we must take note of the many hints Forster gives about the development of their love. Very early, we saw how Margaret defended Henry's physical appearance against Aunt Juley's strictures, and during the account of their meeting on Chelsea embankment we read:

> She had always maintained that Mr. Wilcox had a charm. In times of sorrow or emotion his inadequacy had pained her, but it was pleasant to listen to him now, and to watch his thick brown moustache and high forehead confronting the stars. (Chapter XV)

And even in the very last chapter, after all that has happened, when Helen says 'Meg, may I tell you something? I like Henry.' Margaret replies 'You'd be odd if you didn't.' They get on well together, conversation is never difficult and Margaret finds in his confidence and optimism, his view of life so different from her own, an engaging challenge. Nor are we just told that this is so: we can observe it in all their encounters.

Secondly we must bear in mind what kind of novel Forster is writing, within what convention it is framed. Generally speaking, it is in the realistic tradition, but an absolute realism is neither intended nor required. This is especially true in the matter of sexual relationship, so prominent in the realism of many twentieth-century novels, from Lawrence onward, and although we may be forgiven for speculating on the details of Margaret's married state, it is no part of Forster's purpose to satisfy such interest. He is content that the matter should remain a mystery, as it does when we contemplate so many marriage partnerships in the real life around us. Thus, after the stilted proposal at Ducie Street, when Forster says 'On leaving him she realized that the central radiance had been love', he hopes we will accept that neither Margaret nor the reader has been deceived.

From this point forward Margaret and Henry cause their author no further difficulty; indeed, their characters fit comfortably into his plan: 'Henry did not encourage romance, and she was no girl to fidget for it.' Her love, like so many women's, is nourished and directed by her husband's need. As she interprets it, his need is to learn how to build the rainbow bridge, and her task did not seem so difficult: 'She need trouble him with no gift of her own. She would only point out the salvation that was latent in his own soul, and in the soul of every man.' (Chapter XXII). It is much more difficult than she supposes, however; she fails, as at the outset Forster told us she would, and on two occasions she nearly gives up the attempt. The first, after Jacky's revelation, causes her great anguish, but it is the need to protect the man she is to marry that makes her write with uncharacteristic harshness to Helen. Who would question Forster's insight here? 'Unworthiness', he says, 'stimulates woman. It brings out her deeper nature, for good or for evil. . . . Henry must be forgiven, and made better by love; nothing else mattered.' (Chapter XXVIII). The second occasion brings her face to face with her failure, when Henry refuses to see the connection between his own past situation and Helen's present one, and after Leonard's death she decides to leave her husband. Now her sister's need is the greater. But the law seizes Charles and strikes down his father, so that he will never again resume the life of telegrams and anger. When the novel ends Margaret has succeeded in another task. She has, in Helen's phrase, 'picked up the pieces and made a home', a home for the two people whom she loved in such different ways and whose need of her provided fulfilment. In this last scene, I think for the first time, Forster calls Margaret 'Mrs. Wilcox'. Paul has accidentally kicked the paint on the front door:

> Mrs. Wilcox gave a little cry of annoyance. She did not like anything scratched; she stopped in the hall to take Dolly's boa and gloves out of a vase.

We think for a moment of Ruth Wilcox, who would have been well suited to the task Margaret is performing at the close of the novel. She would never have attempted the other—the salvation of Henry's soul.

This sketch of Margaret's character in action is necessarily incomplete; Forster provides a multitude of clues and chains, here as elsewhere, which the reader will have followed for himself. But one small point attracts curious attention: Margaret disliked babies. Why does Forster add this detail? It is not at all out of character; indeed, her refusal to speak baby-talk to them is at one with her slightly 'blue-stocking' turn of mind. But why bother to make the point? The answer, of course, is in Forster's structural plan. Margaret has no children; for the reason she gives, she is thankful to have none, and so, symbolically, it is Leonard's child who is to inherit Howards End.

Helen's portrait is much less complex than Margaret's,

though a more colourful one. Her romantic nature, her mercurial and impulsive behaviour, her surrender to mystery are consistently represented in all she says and does. The opening letters telling of her immediate response to the Wilcoxes and to Paul; her equally sudden reaction against those she had found so attractive; the incident of the umbrella; the instinctive and passionate fear of the consequences of Margaret's marriage; the visit to Shropshire and all that happens afterwards, right up to her whim of spending the night in Howards End with Margaret— in all these the same character appears. Yet in the centre of everything stands one great stumbling block: would she, despite everything we have seen of her, really have surrendered herself to Leonard? Well, she might. Of Leonard's part in the affair something must be said later, but it is on account of Helen, whom we feel we know so much more intimately than Leonard, that we experience a critical uneasiness. Certainly her surrender is as necessary to the plot as Margaret's marriage, and in that respect it is inevitable, but is there the same justification as there was for the marriage, in terms of character and of the novel's conventions? Perhaps because of those very conventions the reader feels that he has been cheated a little, that although he has not been asked to accept the impossible, and the surprise, when it comes later, is dramatically effective, he has not been fairly prepared for it and too much has been left to his imagination. It is true that his suspicions may have been aroused during Helen's long and mysterious absence, but nothing of the conversation recorded between Helen and Leonard in the coffee-room of the Oniton hotel, after Jacky had gone to bed, gave the slightest pointer to this conclusion, and Helen's realization of what Jacky had been to Henry

made such a conclusion less likely, not more. Later, at
Howards End, when Helen tells Margaret what happened
and Forster is no longer constrained to secrecy for the sake
of the plot, he offers us scant motivation beyond Helen's
loneliness and her feeling that she had snubbed Leonard
a little. He even adds to our difficulties: 'Right up to the
end we were Mr. Bast and Miss Schlegel.' Later still,
possibly because he is conscious that the reader may yet
be in difficulty, to the comments on Leonard's acute
remorse he adds a paragraph about Helen's having been
warped at the time by distasteful memories of Evie's
wedding, but the difficulty is still not adequately resolved.
The reader does not ask for the when, the where and the
how, but he may well think he has a right to a fuller answer
when he asks 'Why?' The secret could have been kept as
long as was necessary, but a retrospective scene might
have been provided to demonstrate the author's con-
tinued dramatic command over his characters. Curiously
enough, however, Helen herself survives this structural
blemish almost unscathed; her later attitude to Leonard,
and after his death to his fading memory and his child, is
in perfect harmony with all that we know of her.

Leonard is the most exacting task of portraiture Forster
undertakes in *Howards End* and some readers believe
that it has not been altogether successfully executed;
some uncertainty of touch in Leonard's dialogue with
Jacky has already been noted. But it must be remembered
that the plan of the novel can allow him only limited
space, for he must not take a central position in our
interest, and within these limits Forster employs a variety
of methods. The characterization is not in the least flat.
His edginess and lack of confidence are tellingly presented
in his first speech:

'Excuse me,' said Margaret's young man, who had for some time been preparing a sentence, 'but that lady has, quite inadvertently, taken my umbrella.' (Chapter V)

He has constantly been obliged to defend himself against the unknown, but when Margaret invites him to walk round with her to collect the umbrella he decides that 'Wickham Place, W., though a risk, was as safe as most things, and he would risk it.' The Schlegel house is to be the scene of two unforgettable episodes, the first when he talks, embarrassingly but with exultation, about the books he has read to lift him from the edge of the abyss. The shattering frankness of his simple 'No' in reply to Helen's question 'But was the dawn wonderful?' reveals the turmoil and bewilderment besetting his whole experience of life. The second episode, of his passionate outburst against the Schlegels when they are advising him to leave the Porphyrion, is an equally successful realization in dramatic form, while the narrative of his nightmare visions before the last journey of his life, and of the senseless chaos of his death, shows Forster's control in a contrasting context. Despite his failure to come to grips with the world around him, Leonard is a figure of pathetic dignity: his immediate rejection of Helen's cheque commands respect, the more so because he knows that the only alternative is to beg charity of his resentful relatives. His part with Helen at Oniton, though not more fully explained than hers with him, makes less demand upon our understanding and we may be more safely left to conjecture the effect upon him of the warmth of 'his Miss Schlegel's' sudden responsiveness.

Little may be said about Henry. He is not a flat

character: we are shown too many aspects of his nature to summarize them in one sentence, but he has not the capacity to surprise the reader. No mystery attaches to him, nothing to invite reflection after the novel has been read. He is successfully drawn in all aspects but one: we can never feel his charm, as we ought to do since even Helen proves susceptible to it at last. It is not that Forster makes him too crudely into a personification of Wilcoxism—that is rather to be Charles's fate—but that his practical common sense, and easy good nature when the wind is fair, are less apparent than his shortcomings. We could forgive him for not noticing things; we forgive him, as Margaret does, for his cheap little sexual adventure. That he could succumb, ten years before at all events, to passionate feeling, however deplorable, may even engage a little of our sympathy. But we cannot forgive him for his blind duplicity, shown even in minor matters such as his dealings in connection with the Ducie Street house and Oniton Grange; nor for his priggishness; nor, ulti- mately, for his inability to distinguish, even in his own wife, between the saviour of his soul and a blackmailer. So the broken and emasculated figure at the end of the novel does not much disturb the idyll. A glance of pity, perhaps, is his due, but we are more concerned with 'such a crop of hay as never'.

Two characters remain, to whom special consideration must be given: Mrs. Wilcox and Miss Avery. They may be considered together, for in one sense they are inseparable from each other. Mrs. Wilcox is more a spirit than a woman and in this respect she is kindred with Mrs. Moore of *A Passage to India*. She gives expression to the spirit of Howards End, the dominant spirit of the novel. Trailing her long dress over the sopping grass, her hands full of hay, stooping down to smell her flowers, she strikes us almost as an earth symbol, a classical goddess of fertility. In her dealings with everyday life she is enigmatic, 'a woman of undefinable rarity', whose thoughts are impenetrable; we get only occasional hints as their course changes. She loves and cares for her family, yielding always to their requirements, but Howards End is deep in the foundations of her soul:

'I suppose you have a garage there?'
'Yes. My husband built a little one only last month, to the west of the house, not far from the wych-elm, in what used to be the paddock for the pony.'
The last words had an indescribable ring about them.
(Chapter VIII)

She knew she was dying. Her pencilled note bequeathing Howards End to Margaret was no passing fancy but an attempt to ensure that the house would receive its spiritual heir. Despite the symbolic emphasis upon her, however, she is wholly convincing; the impression she makes is full of mystery, but it is not vague.

Miss Avery, on the other hand, is a device. Her kind is still to be found, doubtless, among somewhat eccentric old women, especially in the country, but we need not concern ourselves with her as a human being. She is a voice for Howards End when Mrs. Wilcox is no more and the action centres once again upon the house. Her mistaking Margaret for Ruth has nothing to do with physical appearance, nor with the 'bunch of weeds' that Margaret clutched in her hand. Miss Avery knows all about Margaret, and Mrs. Wilcox's wishes, and the past and the future. How she knows is of no importance.

'Did you take her for a spook?' asked Dolly, for whom 'spooks' and 'going to church' summarized the unseen. (Chapter XXIV)

Margaret's reply is significant: 'Not exactly.' Forster deliberately confuses the story of Miss Avery's early friendship with Mrs. Wilcox and the Howard family, giving us only Dolly's incoherent version. But we learn that Miss Avery had refused an offer of marriage from Ruth's brother—or uncle—and he had been killed. 'Tom Howard—he was the last of them.' Tom, we notice, is also the name of the small boy who comes to Howards End while Helen and Margaret are there, and figures in the final scene in the meadow. For the Wilcoxes, Miss Avery is only a silly old farm woman whose expensive wedding-gift to Evie must be returned, lest she presume equality with them. For the reader this is so clearly not her rôle that he is not in the least inclined to ponder by what clairvoyance she arranged Margaret's furniture in Howards End and brushed aside all remonstrance. Her final materialization betrays the eternal presence of the unseen:

'Yes, murder's enough,' said Miss Avery, coming out of the house with the sword.

Questions

1. Show how their reactions to the Wilcox family reveal and distinguish the characters of Margaret and Helen.

2. Discuss the varied methods Forster employs in presenting any one important character in the novel.

3. Consider either the universal appeal of the characters in *Howards End*, or their interest as representative of early twentieth-century society.

4. What limitations do you find in Forster's portrayal of character?

IV: CRITICAL EXAMINATION OF CHAPTERS XIX AND XXXVIII

This series of 'Notes on English Literature' has usually included a detailed study of part of the chosen text, attempting to illustrate the author's creative process as he writes. Reading a novel for the first time it is often difficult, if the novel is a good one, to exercise due restraint over our interest in what happens next, and so we neglect much that is relevant to understanding the whole work. This may not, indeed, be such a bad thing: the author may well be forming our response partly by communicating with inferior levels of our consciousness. Consequently, when we have finished reading, we are aware of the impression the book has made but we may not realize exactly how it has been made, and we like it the better on that account. Critical appreciation, however, involves looking into the writer's workshop. Some workshops are disappointing—a few gadgets, a few pots of paint—and others are fascinating but too elaborately equipped, so that we begin to suspect the craftsman cares more for his refined tools than for what he makes with them. The best books always seem to have written themselves.

Such a study of any chapter of *Howards End* would be revealing, but let us look at a chapter in which the tone is subdued and contrast it with one of crisis.

Although Chapter XIX includes an outburst of passion, it is in general a reflective chapter, a pause in the progress of the story, during which Forster takes stock and Margaret ponders on the future now held out to her. In the previous chapter, it will be remembered, she had gone to London

to discuss with Mr. Wilcox his offer of a house; instead
she received his proposal of marriage. She has given
him no answer yet and Helen, Aunt Juley and Tibby,
waiting at Swanage for Margaret's decision about Ducie
Street, know nothing of Mr. Wilcox's proposal.

'If one wanted to show a foreigner England . . .'
The chapter begins as if it had no more to do with
Forster's story than that famous one beginning 'Seven
miles to the north of Venice . . .' The opening paragraph
is a description of the view from the Purbeck Hills,
expressed, it must be admitted, in rather grandly romantic
terms: all the wild lands come tossing down from Dor-
chester, the sky is 'lucent', Southampton is 'hostess to
the nations' and 'the island will guard the Island's purity
to the end of time'. There is even an echo of Genesis:
'chalk of our chalk, turf of our turf'. The paragraph,
however, marks a change of the narrator's tone, a taking-
in of new breath before continuing his tale; it reminds
us that the little affairs of man are played out against a
more lasting setting, but one not wholly safe from his
disfiguring hand. The Stock Exchange is not far away.
But the strain is of a higher mood and Forster soon
forsakes it for his more familiar comic irony:

> So Frieda Mosebach . . . was brought up to these
> heights to be impressed and, after a prolonged gaze,
> she said that the hills were more swelling here than in
> Pomerania, which was true, but did not seem to Mrs.
> Munt apposite.

An Anglo-German debate of droll patriotism ensues between Frieda and Aunt Juley, who defends the mud of Poole
Harbour against the tideless Baltic on the ground that
water is less unhealthy when it moves about. Windermere

and Grasmere are excused from movement because
they are not salt, and when Frieda counters with the
stink of the fresh water in which her brother-in-law,
Victor, kept his tadpoles, Helen attempts to disengage
the combatants by pointing out the impropriety of
Frieda's vocabulary. Not until Mrs. Munt introduces the
'valuable oyster fishery' which is dependent on the mud
of Poole Harbour does the practical German girl concede
the argument, and another 'international incident' is
peaceably concluded. All this time the reader may well
have been thinking of Margaret returning from London
and now the smoke from her train is seen circling the
harbour.

The conversation is still trivial, but it returns to the
story:

> 'Oh, dearest Margaret, I do hope she won't be
> overtired.'
> 'Oh, I do wonder—I do wonder whether she's
> taken the house.'
> 'I hope she hasn't been hasty.'
> 'So do I—oh, *so* do I.'
> 'Will it be as beautiful as Wickham Place?' Frieda
> asked.

There is some compression in what follows, as if Forster
wished to recall the events of nearly three years ago, both
to the reader and to these characters who are so soon to
be involved once again with the Wilcoxes. Helen is
explaining about Ducie Street:

> '. . . but it's really for Evie that he went there, and
> now that Evie's going to be married—'

and Frieda's interjected 'Ah!' is capable of more than one interpretation. Helen is not in doubt, however:

> 'You've never seen Miss Wilcox, Frieda. How absurdly matrimonial you are!'

Again, Frieda's comment is ambiguous: 'But sister to that Paul?' (How, exactly, is she thinking of Paul?) but there is no ambiguity from Aunt Juley:

> 'And to that Charles', said Mrs. Munt with feeling. 'Oh, Helen, Helen, what a time that was!'

Helen's reply is to reproaches or misgivings that have not been voiced:

> 'Meg and I haven't got such tender hearts. If there's a chance of a cheap house, we go for it.'

In such ways does our own conversation dart and hover; Forster has guided their words and our thoughts to the past, with no sacrifice of naturalness, and all the time Margaret's train and Margaret's marriage draw nearer.

Another and less impressive view opens before us; the train stops; Margaret is to transfer to the pony-cart in which Tibby and a tea-basket are awaiting her. Still Forster is in no hurry. There is more talk, of houses occupied by Wilcoxes ('I wish we could get Howards End,' says Helen. 'That was something like a dear little house.'—Forster is suiting his pattern to his theme) and of the possibility still of Helen's marrying Paul. Helen's rebuttal is characteristically light of tone:

> 'The Great Wilcox Peril will never return. If I'm certain of anything it's of that.'

Frieda's comment, 'One is certain of nothing but the

truth of one's own emotions', provides the opportunity
for a reflective paragraph before Margaret appears. The
comment is one of the variants on Keats's 'I am certain
of nothing but of the holiness of the heart's affections,
and the truth of the imagination' which H. A. Smith
has pointed out. It is hardly surprising that it should come
to Forster's mind at this juncture, when Margaret is about
to make her great decision in the face of Helen's intuitive
fears. It is a little unexpected on Frieda's lips, but it
would be impossible on Aunt Juley's and if he had said
it himself it would have seemed to cast prophetic doubt
on Helen's assertion. In the event, he links it with Frieda
to good effect:

> The remark fell damply on the conversation. But
> Helen slipped her arm round her cousin, somehow
> liking her the better for making it. It was not an original
> remark, nor had Frieda appropriated it passionately,
> for she had a patriotic rather than a philosophic mind.
> Yet it betrayed that interest in the universal which the
> average Teuton possesses and the average Englishman
> does not. It was, however illogically, the good, the
> beautiful, the true, as opposed to the respectable, the
> pretty, the adequate.

He concludes with one of those ominous hints he drops so
frequently: 'It may have been a bad preparation for what
followed.'

Now the awaited moment is upon us. Three times in
two lines the words 'the pony-cart coming' are repeated.
For a little longer expectation is held, while we glimpse
the scene again: the budding lanes, the highroad, the saddle
and the track 'at right angles along the ridge of the down'.
A few excited exchanges and 'Margaret came close up

to her and whispered that she had had a proposal of marriage from Mr. Wilcox.' Helen is at first amused, but as she stands, preoccupied with holding open the gate, the truth dawns, and with a hurried word to Aunt Juley and Frieda, she turns to Margaret and bursts into tears. Helen's passion bursts in frantic repetition of 'Don't!' Panic and emptiness return. Margaret misunderstands, surprisingly, thinking that Helen is contemplating the loss of her sister; even more surprising from Margaret is the thought implicit in 'when there has seemed a chance of her marrying', but of such irrepressible thoughts are misunderstandings born. Emotion is heightened by a touch of descriptive detail, almost musical in its effect, as Margaret follows her sister 'through the wind that gathers at sundown on the northern slopes of hills'. As stupidity seizes her momentarily, and the immense landscape is blurred, the passion subsides, reason regains control and the two girls sit down to quieter talk. Margaret gives an account of her developing attachment to Henry. She does not invoke romance; she frankly admits that love is only now beginning to form part of her feeling. Helen can do no more than grope through the recurrent nightmare of her experience with Paul, the horror of telegrams and anger, all her earlier lighthearted confidence dissipated in her anxiety for Margaret. Again we have the sense of pattern and rhythm, of the organic importance to the whole novel of the opening scenes at Howards End.

Margaret begins to speak with objective clear-sightedness of Mr. Wilcox's shortcomings, in the hope of re-assuring Helen that the sister on whose leadership she and Tibby have always relied has not taken leave of her understanding. For a short paragraph Forster interrupts, to step forward in time, foreshadowing the inevitable

E

change that marriage will effect on his heroine and dis-pelling, as if incidentally, any doubt the reader may still entertain as to whether or not the marriage is in fact to take place. For a moment there is a view of a more distant horizon, and then Margaret continues, warming to her theme of the usefulness of Wilcoxes in every age.

> 'There are times when it seems to me—'
> 'And to me, and to all women. So one kissed Paul.'
> 'That's brutal,' said Margaret. Mine is an absolutely different case. I've thought things out.'
> 'It makes no difference thinking things out. They come to the same.'
> 'Rubbish!'
> There was a long silence, during which the tide returned into Poole Harbour. 'One would lose some-thing', murmured Helen, apparently to herself.

And so the dialogue ends.

There remains a coda, in which we are directed once again to look at England from the Purbeck Hills, but this time we are not showing it to a foreigner:

> For what end are her fair complexities, her changes of soil, her sinuous coast? Does she belong to those who have moulded her and made her feared by other lands, or to those who have added nothing to her power, but have somehow seen her, seen the whole island at once, lying as a jewel in a silver sea, sailing as a ship of souls, with all the brave world's fleet accom-panying her towards eternity?

The chapter is complete, closing, as it began, with the broad view of England. It could have been omitted without any interruption of narrative continuity; its central dramatic moment is not crucial. It is an interlude only, but its importance to tempo and theme can scarcely be over-stressed. Margaret has stated the case for connection, no longer as a liberal theory but as the key to the personal conduct of her life. She has made her decision and in the next chapter Mr. Wilcox becomes Henry.

Chapter XXXVIII is very different from Chapter XIX. Instead of reflection and a pause in the movement there is critical conflict; events are enacted not against the wide suggestiveness of a great English panorama but over a couple of garden chairs; variety of subject and mood give place to the exclusive concentration of two people grappling with each other on the edge of a spiritual precipice, towards which they are driven, like all who quarrel, by an incomprehensible power. Here is not discussion, but the turn of the screw.

The method is almost wholly dramatic, such additions as there are to the dialogue between Margaret and Henry being merely of the nature of stage directions. The movement is relentlessly from quiet beginnings to the terrifying climax. The conclusion is impasse and despair. Yet all this occurs without any distortion of the characters of these two people as they have appeared throughout the novel; there is no dramatic 'unmasking', none of the sensationalism of a common row. Henry speaks from first to last with the dignified restraint which often comes so easily to the undeveloped heart; Margaret's passion burns with the clear flame of reason and vision.

'The tragedy began quietly enough.' The chapter opens with yet another of Forster's ominous hints. The nature of the tragedy we can hardly guess, its accom-paniment of death and imprisonment and broken manhood quite beyond our present view. In retrospect, however, we can see that Forster is not thinking of tragedy as the final assessment, for though it enters the lives of all the central characters in various ways, it is a part of experience, not the sum. When, therefore, he speaks of 'the' tragedy he is primarily recalling the word used just before the end of the previous chapter: 'the sense of tragedy closed in on Margaret again as soon as she left the house'.

Helen has suggested that she and Margaret should spend the night together at Howards End and Margaret, a loyal wife, comes to Charles's house to seek her husband's permission. How much the granting of this request means to Helen, and therefore to Margaret, may be measured by the change that Howards End and the Wickham Place furniture have already effected on the unhappy girl. Helen had at first seemed almost a stranger to her sister, but by the end of the previous chapter the old relationship had been re-established. Helen would have stayed without leave, but one senses that Margaret wants her husband's understanding support rather than his permission. She wants to believe him capable of connecting. Henry, however, is in an unpromising mood; it is a situation for Wilcox decisiveness. The cab-driver is given short shrift, and Dolly is abruptly ordered to wheel the baby's perambulator away; for a moment there is a touch of comic irony: 'Baby was wheeled out of earshot, and did not hear about the crisis till later years.' Margaret's chance of success is slender; it is now *her* turn.

Henry intends to use only sweet reason and gentleness towards his wife. He is full of appropriately sententious clichés: he is 'a man of the world', Helen is 'more sinned against than sinning' and he has 'some experience of life'.

At the same time he must consider his 'position in society' and, if necessary, some unknown person must be 'thrashed within an inch of his life'. The worn currency stands in a neat pile, each counter ready for use as required. The early part of the dialogue is given a double interest because Margaret is not allowed an opportunity to make her request, and the reader can see how every stage of Henry's catechism lowers her spirits and makes her request more difficult.

He begins with the need for 'absolute honesty and plain speech' and this is enough to make Margaret bend her head; in a moment he has distinguished himself from 'your Bernard Shaws who consider nothing sacred', claimed the right to speak as a husband and praised her as 'a most exceptional woman'. All Margaret's senses forsake her; she blushes at his insensibility, but he mistakes the blush for embarrassment about Helen and, growing still more kind, he says: I see that you feel as I felt when—' leaving unfinished the reference to Helen in the porch of Howards End. When Margaret stammers her 'No' to the enquiry about a wedding ring there is an appalling silence. Margaret desperately tries to embark on her mission, but he waves her interruption aside: 'One point at a time.' Helen's 'seducer' must be identified. She rises to her feet, her face ashen. He urges his point with gentle authority, pressing her to be seated again. The icy irrelevance of her reply is lost on him: 'I like to stand, if you don't mind, for it gives me a pleasant view of the Six Hills.' When he reveals that he has already involved Charles and Tibby, anger begins to replace her stunned dismay and she strikes back.

'Are we to make her seducer marry her?' she asked.
'If possible. Yes.'

'But, Henry, suppose he turned out to be married already? One has heard of such cases.'

'In that case he must pay heavily for his misconduct, and be thrashed within an inch of his life.'

She is glad, for once, that Henry cannot connect, for she had put both their lives in danger and he had not noticed. Exhausted, she at last puts Helen's request to him.

'It was the crisis of his life.' Once again the reader is conscious of the pressure of plot upon character. Would Henry really have made any bones about such a simple and harmless request? Might he not rather have contented himself with disapproval, pointing out the advantages of a comfortable hotel, but without insistence? If he had allowed him to do so, however, Forster would have lost the occasion for this final confrontation between Margaret and Henry, this ultimate failure to connect, and it is symbolically necessary that Howards End itself should be involved. Yet before we charge Forster with awkward contrivance we should notice how thoroughly he has prepared the psychological situation. At a moment when Henry is enjoying the confident control, as he supposes, of an affair that calls for the utmost Wilcox experience, he is taken off guard. As so often happens in disputes of this kind, before he has really made up his mind he has entrenched himself behind argument and provoked Margaret into so widening the scope of debate that in the end he is concerned only to defend his own position. Reason, a sense of proportion and Helen's unaccountable whim must all be sacrificed to the greater cause. Too late, Margaret realizes all this:

Again she would have recalled the words as soon as they were uttered. She had not led up to them with sufficient care. She longed to warn him that they were far more important than he supposed.

She tries hard, pleading Helen's character and present position, but hyprocrisy is now blinding him: 'a house in which one has once lived becomes in a sort of way sacred'. This seems to him a weightier argument than that Helen will catch cold. Then he thinks of another: 'If she wants to sleep one night, she may want to sleep two. We shall never get her out of the house, perhaps.' Anger increases Margaret's recklessness and she allows herself to be sidetracked. 'Would it matter?' she asks, and immediately retreats, insisting that the request is for one night only. She would of course stay with her sister. This he positively forbids, not because of the damp house, but because she must be on hand to meet Charles, who is concerned as the future owner of Howards End.

> 'In what way? Will Helen's condition depreciate the property?'

Margaret's searing irony brings the precipice still nearer, but she makes a final effort:

> 'Will you forgive her—as you hope to be forgiven, and as you have actually been forgiven? Forgive her for one night only. That will be enough.'

Now Henry is forced into a position of siege. Rejecting the truth as it begins to glimmer upon him, he cants with the memory of his 'dear wife' and gives his final refusal. Nothing can restrain Margaret further. Her last hope, not of fulfilling Helen's trivial desire, but of achieving the whole purpose of her marriage to this man, even of salvaging something from the wreck, has been consumed in these angry flames. In every line of her denunciation, in all its staccato rhythms, the burden of her heart is released. Henry's reply, with its carefully chosen vocabulary—'I perceive you are attempting blackmail . . . my rule through life has been . . . I can only repeat . . .'— is as true an expression of his outraged self-esteem as Margaret's words had been of her passion.

The final paragraph is of the silence following some shattering disaster. She looses her hands from his, which he wipes, with deliberation and a too-obvious symbolism, on his handkerchief as he goes into the house. Margaret stands drained of feeling, looking at the Six Hills, tombs of Danish soldiers, at once sentinels over the past and, in their spring growth, harbingers of the future. They bring back a perspective.

This magnificently controlled scene must surely be Forster's finest passage of sustained dramatic writing, worthy of comparison with the best of its kind in modern literature. Throughout the chapter we are made aware of the speakers' characters, of all that has gone before, of the unspoken thoughts behind their words. We scarcely need Forster's occasional references to the precipice, for we can see it so clearly that we tremble ourselves. Little wonder that Forster's novels attract the attention of playwrights. In such scenes as this he leaves them nothing to do.

Questions

1. Choose two contrasting chapters, and write a critical commentary on them to show Forster's mastery of the novelist's techniques.

2. Discuss the importance of a single chapter of your own choice in relation to the whole novel.

3. What contribution to *Howards End* is made by (*a*) the presentation of the English scene, (*b*) dramatic dialogue, (*c*) philosophical reflection?

4. Consider the nature and function of the comedy in *Howards End*.

5. '*Howards End* bears too great a burden of symbolism.' Discuss.

V. ACHIEVEMENT

Howards End has been read and esteemed for nearly sixty years. It is not a popular novel: one cannot imagine it holding the imagination and interest of a great reading public throughout serial publication, in the manner of a work by Dickens or Hardy, for Forster is not a popular novelist in the commonly accepted sense. But it is clearly one of the major novels of the twentieth century, and its appeal and influence have not been limited to a coterie of 'intellectual' readers. Forster has reached a much larger public than has Virginia Woolf, his early contemporary.

His general readers speak of *Howards End* with great affection. It has meant something to them, and not only to those of them for whom its scenes recall personal reminiscence of the Edwardian age; it expresses liberal ideas, a gentle and civilized humanism essentially optimistic in tone, with its suggestion that it is within the power of people of goodwill and intelligence to counter the depredations of an increasingly materialistic age.

Literary critics, on the other hand, while acknowledging Forster's importance and according particular respect to *Howards End*, have qualified their judgments in various ways. Some regard it as primarily a realistic novel in which the symbolism is intrusive; others, as a symbolic morality unbalanced by too much vivid realism. It is praised for its humanity, for its poetic vision, and adversely criticized for its disregard of probability in the pursuit of its themes. The end, especially, has been found too idyllic and contrived, too facile a solution to the problems of personal relationship that the novel has so faithfully exhibited. These judgments all depend on some preconceived idea of what a novel should be and although one may recognize some justice in them one nevertheless feels that they are unimportant, that the imaginative truth of the whole transcends all such considerations. To understand this truth we must be prepared to follow Forster along various 'planes of reality'. The phrase is E. M. W. Tillyard's in his book *Shakespeare's Last Plays* and, after due allowance has been made for the different conventions appropriate to poetic drama and to the novel, it may be argued that *Howards End* demands a multiplicity of response similar to that required for *The Tempest* or *The Winter's Tale*. This refusal of Forster's to conform to a single convention throughout is part of the characteristic elusiveness which was noticed at the outset of this essay and which is his most distinctive feature. He will not pretend, as some novelists (Conrad, for example) labour so painfully to do, that he is merely a recorder of events.

For this reason *Howards End* is not dated, nor is it likely to become so: it is not a period piece in anything except external details. It gives a picture of Edwardian manners and scenes but they are not of first importance. Future readers will respond as readily as their predecessors to its presentation of the importance of human relations, of their subtlety and difficulty, their dangers and rewards; to the stringency of its comic irony; to the sympathy and warmth of the author's personality, evident in all he writes. These are the qualities that make it satisfying to read Forster's novels again and again.

He is not a 'great' novelist, however, and *Howards End* is not a 'great 'novel, to use with cautious qualification the adjective so easy to apply and so difficult to define. The reason is not simply that his range is limited and his output small (Jane Austen achieved greatness with only one more novel and an even narrower range) but he lacks the broad popular appeal and the clear, recognizable voice of the great novelists; his novels have not the dominant urgency of George Eliot's or Hardy's or Lawrence's; and his preference for intelligent compromise makes him seem a patient but oddly sequestered spectator rather than a participant in the common struggle.

Forster's literary indebtedness, like that of all original writers, is difficult to trace, and his own words in a B.B.C. broadcast, *The Legacy of Samuel Butler* (June 1952), must here suffice:

> Samuel Butler influenced me a great deal . . . He, Jane Austen and Marcel Proust are the three authors who have helped me most over my writing, and he did more than the other two to help me look at life the way I do.

The extent of others' indebtedness to him is equally hard to guess. Perhaps it is still too soon to see his influence clearly, but although he has no obvious successor, it is certain that a writer whose work has been admired from the earliest years of this century, and today more than ever is receiving world-wide critical attention, has earned a distinguished place in English literary history.

FURTHER READING

E. M. Forster: The four other novels will all be found helpful to a deeper understanding of *Howards End*, but especially *The Longest Journey* and *A Passage to India*. The collected short stories reveal Forster's interest in the use of fantasy.

The essays gathered in *Abinger Harvest* and *Two Cheers for Democracy* express a wide range of his views on literature and life, and *Aspects of the Novel* is invaluable to all students of novels generally and Forster's in particular.

Criticism: There is now a considerable amount of critical writing on E. M. Forster, and it is possible here to give only a few titles chosen from the works available.

The most recent full-length assessment is by an American, Wilfred Stone, *The Cave and the Mountain* (Stanford University Press and Oxford University Press, 1966). *The Achievement of E. M. Forster* by J. B. Beer (Chatto and Windus, 1962) is also a major study, while the shorter work by K. W. Gransden, *E. M. Forster*, appeared in the same year in the *Writers and Critics* series (Oliver and Boyd). The most important of the earlier critical works is Lionel Trilling's *E. M. Forster—a study* (Hogarth Press, 1944). A full list was provided by Malcolm Bradbury in his essay *A Short Guide to Forster Studies*, published in *The Critical Survey* of Summer 1965, and Bradbury has also edited a collection of critical essays on Forster, including earlier views by I. A. Richards, F. R. Leavis and others, as well as more modern judgments, in his volume in the *Twentieth Century Views* series (Prentice-Hall, 1966).

NOTES ON ENGLISH LITERATURE

Chief Adviser: JOHN D. JUMP, *Professor of English Literature in the University of Manchester*

General Editor: W. H. MASON, *Sometime Senior English Master, The Manchester Grammar School*

1 Shakespeare **Macbeth**
   JOHN HARVEY
2 Chaucer **The Prologue**
   R. W. V. ELLIOTT, *Professor of English, Flinders University, South Australia*
3 T. S. Eliot **Murder in the Cathedral**
   W. H. MASON
4 Austen **Pride and Prejudice**
   J. DALGLISH, *Sometime Senior English Master, Tiffin School*
5 Shakespeare **Twelfth Night**
   BARBARA HARDY, *Professor of English, Birkbeck College*
7 Emily Brontë **Wuthering Heights**
   BARBARA HARDY
8 Hardy **The Mayor of Casterbridge**
   G. G. URWIN, *Senior English Master, Sale Grammar School for Boys*
9 Charlotte Brontë **Jane Eyre**
   BARBARA HARDY
10 Shaw **St. Joan**
   W. H. MASON
11 Conrad **Nostromo**
   C. B. COX, *Professor of English Literature, University of Manchester*
12 Dryden **Absalom and Achitophel**
   W. GRAHAM, *Sometime Senior English Master, Dame Allan's Boys' School, Newcastle-upon-Tyne*
13 Sheridan **The Rivals, The School for Scandal, The Critic**
   B. A. PHYTHIAN, *Senior English Master, The Manchester Grammar School*
14 Shakespeare **King Lear**
   HELEN MORRIS, *Principal Lecturer in English, Homerton College, Cambridge*

31 Synge **Riders to the Sea, Playboy of the Western World**
A. PRICE, *Senior Lecturer in Education, Queen's University, Belfast*

32 Byron **Childe Harold III and IV, Vision of Judgement**
PATRICIA BALL, *Lecturer in English, Royal Holloway College*

33 Shakespeare **Othello**
G. P. WAKEFIELD

34 Dickens **Bleak House**
P. DANIEL, *Assistant Master, Ratcliffe College, Leicester*

35 Dickens **Hard Times**
GRAHAM HANDLEY

36 Miller **Death of a Salesman**
C. J. PARTRIDGE, *Assistant Professor, Department of English Literature and Language, University of Victoria, B.C., Canada*

37 Shakespeare **Hamlet**
KEITH SAGAR, *Staff Tutor, Extra Mural Dept., University of Manchester*

38 Hopkins **The Poetry of Gerard Manley Hopkins**
H. C. SHERWOOD, *Senior Staff Tutor, Extra Mural Dept., University of Manchester*

39 Milton **Paradise Lost I & II**
W. RUDDICK, *Lecturer in English Literature, University of Manchester*

40 Greene **Brighton Rock**
A. PRICE

41 Joyce **A Portrait of the Artist as a Young Man**
CHRISTOPHER HANSON

42 Conrad **Lord Jim**
D. L. MENSFORTH

43 Austen **Mansfield Park**
R. A. COX, *Assistant Master, Manchester Grammar School*

44 Shakespeare **Coriolanus**
C. J. PARTRIDGE

45 Shakespeare **Romeo and Juliet**
HELEN MORRIS

46 Jonson **Volpone and The Alchemist**
MORRIS VENABLES, *Senior Lecturer in English, Redland College, Bristol*

47 Hardy **Tess of the D'Urbervilles**
JULIET MCLAUCHLAN, *Teacher of English, Aylesbury High School*